BLUE BIRD FROM HEAVEN
HEALER OF THE SOULS

BLUE BIRD FROM HEAVEN
HEALER OF THE SOULS

Rubendra Kaushik Bagdash (Darjee)

Bigfoot Publications
Because, there's a writer in everyone.

Blue Bird From Heaven: Healer Of The Souls

Author : Rubendra Kaushik Bagdash (Darjee)

First Published by
Bigfoot06 Publications (OPC) Pvt. Ltd. B-10,12Shree Shyam Palace, Sector 4,5 Chowk, Old Railway Road, Gurugram, Haryana (122001)

Website: www.bigfootpublications.in
Email: info@bigfootpublications.com

First Edition: December 2022

ISBN Print Book - 978-81-960097-0-0

Printed in India

Hakuna Matata **- AFRICA**

Man without women is half man **- INDIAN**

Rubendra Kaushik Badash (Darjee)

Someone who get exhausted doing nothing, One who believe there are no such things as nothing as he finds everything in that nothingness, hollowness, and emptiness. Sometimes these obscure feelings that boils within him make him insane and to remain sane in this insane world he scribbles and twang guitar and sing until his throat ache..

My email id :- rubendra38@gmail.com
Phone number- 9883278528, 9564734787

DEDICATED TO GOD AND GODESSES

WHO ARE LOST IN THE CROWD.

To set them free from an Invisible cage,

&

To give them freedom being free from the matrix and to shower them real love, salvation, mukti and to show the direction to thee! Is the aim, goal, whole purpose of my Art.

Special thanks to my Mom and Dad and all my friends and families, who brought me here in this blue planet.

To my Brother Rupak kundan bagdash and best friend Nova, Who taught me the meaning of something which I never understood but I sniffed love that is why I say they are more than friends.

And to all my teachers I want to spout their names from my intrinsic heart Gopal sir, Rehman sir, Manoj sir, and all Jesuits fathers who taught me in Saint Alphonsus school. Samantakdas, SdG da Partha Da, Sounak da, prabuddha da, debjani di, Kavita ma'am, sujit da SC ma'am etc. And all the underground people who are rotting in a gutter because they direct me to take a course at Ramakrishnan cultural studies institute for appreciation of Indiana art.

Thanks to soumiks sir of Shantiniketan who used to teach in Appreciation of Indian art and used to hypnotize with this wisdom.

Late. Santosh Bagdash & My Mother Rita Bagdash

This book is written by me, for me, and for everyone.

Dedicated to - OM

Hey;

I was just another human being traversing lonely in this peculiar world where time decides the fate of a wo/man. I being just another human being got kicked but somehow from somewhere life lifted me and nurtured me with love and care and out of the blue something happened/spiritual awakening in my life which compelled me to seek and wonder what is that force that makes us breathe automatically, what is that force that passes current from switch to bulb. I guess I looked like a fool, some people called me mad but, that's alright.

Anyway, since then, I kept on seeking something beyond myself; I kept on seeking love and love made me dance, I kept on dancing wild like some lost puppy, lost in the fair looking for shelter and I commenced to find solace in music and books. I started reading mythology, love stories of Durjoy Dutta, Ravindra Singh, Jefferey archer, and Motivational books of Robin Sharma, Shiv Khera but literature kept on sowing seeds somewhere inside my heart and soul. I kept on reading and reading!

I shifted my stream from Commerce to Comparative literature just for the sake of love for literature and Art and

then, Heidegger, Plato, Socrates, Antoine De Saint Exupery, Tagore, Kabir, Meera, Devdutt Pattanaik, Amartya sen, Rumi, Dhansal, Toni Morrison, Kafka, Murakami, Juan Rulfo, Voltaire, Balzac, Tolstoy, Baudelaire, Dante, Edgar Alan Poe, Garcia Marquez, Derrida, Manuel Puig, Fyodor Dostoevsky, Charles Bukowski, Arko Mukherjee, Parvauthy Baul, Fakir, Jhalakman, Luck Devi Sundas, etc started to splash colours in the barrenness of my heart, illuminating light in the darkness of my soul.

They broke the invisible wall and took me somewhere beyond this world and the seeker in me got attracted and compelled me to create a book from everything I wrote secretly hiding from the crowd, for the past 5 years.

I never thought in my wildest dream that it would turn into something beautiful. My poetry is genre-free as I believe it is the voice of the soul written in a trance consciousness and is free from any kind of imitation.

I hope you will at least read once and think! I know my book wouldn't look or come out as a typical poetry book rather it would deconstruct the very stagnant notion of the genre we call poetry, I believe more than poems it is a lyrical verse, more than content and form, I have focused more on the essence(core), so I opted to write it from the mystical dimension.

I don't know how much impact it would make on readers and how much influence it would make to the general public but I believe whoever will hold my book would surely find the vivid light of my spirit and soul and will rise from the matrix and commence to seek something beyond the self. Which I believe is the ultimate purpose of literature.

"BLUEBIRD FROM HEAVEN HEALER OF THE SOUL"

To my Father who art lost in Universe
To my Godfather who was an HealerAnd to my Grandnee who I never saw

Raghu Gurung Hidden gem as a prophet in a birds of valley

The blue bird from heaven is something bigger than Samsara. I'm doing my karma/work and carrying blessings of gods.

In quest of peace and salvation. I'm just an ordinary.

poet claimed by Mr. Rubendra Kaushik Bagdash.

•

But to due to some predicament and societal dogmas ,I'm walking like a lost puppy lost in a fair seeking cookies/Bread.

I'm dying every day because of conflicts between left and right, daily hustle and bustle of peoples still I'm living being a responsible man doing my own thing and living feeling the fresh air.

In the war of love

Only light can win,

Only dumb, deaf and blind;

Can hear it's a mystery,

It's maddening magic!

"Love is its keypad

Only wise can fathom"

And Sometimes I miss her!

. . . . To make her feel love is my intrinsic wish.....

An ode to ;

All broken souls, who laugh without any laughter!

Dedicated :

"To everyone who mocked me and made fun of me Just because I wore cheaper clothes."

We are the sad generation with happy pictures,

We barely converse looking deep into our eyes,

Rather we will to talk through stories

Our understanding of self and other are based on assumptions;

We are insomniacs cause we have the

internet

Our merry depends on memes

Our feeling depends on salaries

We have poisoned our emotion

Our eyes and spirit is caged in the web

We are missing our soul, freedom,

Maybe life too.

I been here all alone today

Got no place to anywhere

I have been crying at night

To hide the sadness of my heart

I know you are surrounded by a wall

But don't forget you can fly.

{Samsara}

We fear, what we don't know

We don't fear what we know

So they don't let us know.

But my comrade! we have to know!

To Harijans

HIDDEN SOUL OF INDIA

For a while let me smell
The scent of your skin
Let me inhale life and exhale love ;
With our closed eyes
Let's us perish,.
Everything that makes us
hard and heavy,
All the things that keep us at bay;

Don't rush! Breathe! Free!
Feel the beat of your own heart
Dance in the beat of your own soul
Feel the life running through your veins
Embrace the whole cosmos,
Embracing you back with thy whole heart
Aww! At that moment we fathom
The real music, magic, mystery
And the beauty of life in this
world

Where we are born to die;

Then we will realize that light

That is within us,

But first, we have to be the light!

HOPELESSNESS

Now, Beat and burn us

Or shoot in our head

Now, Beat and burn us

Or shattered our heart

With all you ammunition

But we won't be scared;

Cause now we are in the street lights,

And you said:

Red is the color of blood my friend but it is the colors of love.

.... To my brothers and sisters who are stranded in the delusional and deserted road........

One who love unconditionally and whose heart is of gold...

LIGHT HAS NO SHADOW!

You have to be light then only you may fathom what this mad poetis trying to portray.

PS= THE VOICE OF THE VOICELESSNESS.

*" **Every word utter with pure love is a prayer**"*

*. . . . . **By- Rubendra Bagdash**...............*

Thy move slow yet thy is fast

Thy is simple, yet so complex

Thy is vulnerable yet so strong

With thy everything make sense

Without thee everything is chaos

Everything is within they say

Yet I seek thee

Like a lost puppy.

There are voices that lingers around me
There are eyes that say different stories
This world tries to play with thy feelings
And I lay like a hungry and homeless man
In the corner of the street
Longing to go home.

THE DESOLATE PARASITE

I can only show;
You must see,
I can only explain;
You must fathom,

I can only show you
The way;
You must walk!

I can only make you feel
You must believe!

No! I just do not want to hug
I want to lose myself, free myself,

No! I just do not want to pour my lust,
I want to feel the essence of whole cosmos;

In a feel of thy touch,

I will wait, I can wait, till you come
To offer me the light of the God.

TO CIVILIZED BEINGS

Learned to fly like birds,
Swim like fish, order food online,
Date with the help of tinder;

Sex robot is coming up,
Hold the whole world in our hand;

Still homeless die in streets
In the coldness of the night,

Spent trillions of dollars building;
Church, temples, mosque, monastery
Still, we kill and die in the name of God;

And we claim ourselves as most civilized animal,
Peculiar us, aren't we?

BROKEN HEARTS

Broken hearts screams, it is an illusion
But soul whispered it is synchronicity,

More than worldly flings
More than mortal love of hearts

He jumps off the cliff, hoping she will too,
Sadly, she did not!

Birds in the sky sang:
New day will dawn,
It is just a matter of time?

He let himself fall,
Hoping she will too
But she never did...

ECLIPSE LOVE

Gone were the days when roller coaster excited me

Now, it feels like time has come to fly high in spaceship,

Gone were the days when love felt like a battle to fought

Now it feels like it is only the place where God resides

Only heart that is pure can feel it is true magic,

Only soul that are not caged here can fathom its mystery

I do not want to force and go against consent of force

As I know:

No one can stop eclipse, Not even the sun,

Nor the moon, Nor me nor can you.

STAY AWAY FROM MAD ONES

They call him mad when he closes all his doors
To be lonely and isolated from society and crowd.

They find him peculiar when he says he does not
believe His family, country, culture but only in the
wholeness,Oneness,

They do not get it when he says he is dancing;
Though his body barley moves, but trust me:

Only the ones who watch can see him
Only the ones who listen can hear him
Only the one who love the self can feel him

And may comprehend voice of a silent guy
Spark of a boring person, beauty beyond the mess
Richness beyond poverty and
Yes, life beyond death.

‘TRAGEDY’

So many lonely souls
craving for sweet company,

So many unhappy lovers,
trying to escape the prison;

What a beautiful tragedy!

DROP OF WATER IN AN OCEAN

I may be laying like a dead fish doing nothing
I may be hovering like a fool, but I feel the system
Rolling in my thoughts, in my head,

I find myself fighting to transcend that feel
With the light I feels within;

Sometimes I may act like a maniac
I turn all my desires into headache,
All my failures into ache of my foot,

Doing so I realized how imperative it has become
Just to sit and feel just to feel;

Everything in you and you in everything.

TO THE SEEKERS

When it rains! everyone carries Jars,
But some of us try to plough
Well for everyone,

Whether, it is love or madness;
That we do not know,
But we must roll on and on!

DAY BY DAY

Oh you! Creators of Art
Oh you! Seeker of the truth

Let reason kills you but do not
Let passion die in you;

Oh Artist! You create/Craft, Art
But do not thou think,

Something is also creating thee?
Day by day, Moment by moment?

CONSTELLATION OF STARS

Even if you shaved your hair,
I keep long beard,

We both turned ugly
Fat or cracked,

It feels as if, we would still be together
It feels as if, you are not my choice;

But we are chosen!

TO THE GIRL WHO RESIDE NEAR YOUTH HOSTEL?

Crosses, thousands of Mountains
Hundreds of seas and ocean,

To run away from a person

But

Who knew? we cannot run away from a person
Who live deep within our heart.

ROUNDABOUT

Roundabout! Roundabout!
Goes round and round, spins on and on

When she goes up, I smile
When she goes down, I feel butterflies

As if, I am not playing but
Being played;

So instead of rushing, I stay calm
To raise the little boy, I have within,

I hope I am living fine, the way I should
As I know, whatever I do,

The roundabout will spin on and on....

SONGS OF BIRDS

A Bird asks-

But why you follow me like crazy?

With you I feel safe and sound,

Complete and free,

More human than robots,

Live more than survive,

Tell me why shouldn't I follow?

The other bird replied! And said:

"Love is unconditional,

It is we; who Conditioned it"

TO DREAMERS

In the darkness we crawl and walk fearlessly
making way for ourselves;

Not only for ourselves but for everyone
to explore life going beyond the horizons,

To bring life from the unexplored infinities
and they call us mad!

A GENTLE REMINDER

Soon we will be gone
Will fade like a shooting star

Suffering will no longer suffocate us
Wealth or fame will no longer define us

We will sway like a beautiful dream
in the vividness of the day,

We will vanish into the unknown
Like the way stars immerse into the black hole

And we will no longer have to prove our worth and lie
just to fit in this crazy word.

CULTURE IS A CULT

Love your culture, Fall in love with your tradition
Be proud of your community, do rituals,

But if it makes you feel like yours is superior
Others are inferior, please stop!

You are doing but you are not, in the doing;
Following without experiencing and realizing,

Laughing without you being in that laughter
Forgetting we are water, whether;

We are in pond, stream, rivulet, river,
Waterfall or in an ocean.

LOVE

Like a star, she glistened so vivid
Smelled so tempting,
He lost himself immersing,

Hunger rose inside his bloodstained heart
Made him yearns for healing and cure,

But voice went dry, Lump got frozen
And she faded like a shooting star

Into the unknown and
In the darkness he waits for her

Like a fish waits for a drop of water in the desert
Just to feel the taste of life for a last time...

SHE IS NATURE

Let me sing the song of our bond
Let this world thrill, let the clouds roars
Let the river swash,

As she is so pure, naïve, and real
From the sky to earth she gazes, cast her spell
Through the twinkles of the stars,

Her voice you may hear in the song of
Cicadas, crickets, and birds

Know her and you will never walk alone
Everyone will become your family, this whole world
Will turn into your home,

You will realize the connections with
Stars, moon, and galaxies.

EARTH IS A TINY CELL

Earth is a tiny cell and our body is a cosmos
Beneath and above billion of stars and galaxies
We may disappear like our own cells in our bodies

Wheel of life was and will spin on and on
Only change is constant here,
This lets everyone new to experience;

Reality is gravity, it holds us, traps us
We end up locking ourselves in a shiny cage,

Some says it is a fate, journey
Destinations, Karma, Drama,
Whatever it is;

All I know is, it is not for nothing but
A chance to feel the essence of everything.

IF EVERYTHING IS AS IT IS?

Trees just a tree, Planets nothing but
Mercury, Venus, Earth, Mars,

Home nothing but four-square wall?
Birth just the outcome of sex?

Sunrise and sunset nothing but
The result of rotations?

Human beings as nothing
But a piece of body, born to suffer and die?

All the suffering, injustice, good and bad
Lessons, experiences, moments, loss

Just for nothing?

THE TRUTH

Alas! The truth will come into the surface
You may use every tactic and power to suppress it
But in the end, it shall arise like a dawn,

Those voices hidden beneath fearful eyes
Will smile like infants without any guile,

Alas! God will laugh, those soul who died
An early grave in selfish propaganda
Will get salvation, widow and orphan will live again

But until we do not realize, all we are looking for is
A little bit of Love, light and peace,

Power will greed soul, humanity will sink, evil will rise
But in the end, those who look will see,

Who will hear will listen, who seeks will find thee.

OTHER SIDE OF GRASS

I am not happy, Nor sad!

I am not rich, Nor I am poor!

I love summer but I do not hate winter

I love blues but I do not make fun of pops

Sometimes I lose my mind

Just to find the self,

I often feel hollow but somehow

I ended up finding fullness in that hollowness

Music in the silence, Meaning in the void

And I feel like may be;

"It's okay! to feel sadness just like happiness,
sometimes".

MEMORIES

Memories flow like waves in ocean
Some phase collides with rocks;

Some sweet and some bitter,
Everyone think/feel I had the best

But the truth is;
Everyone feels the same joy and sorrow

In their own respective ways.

DREAM OF A BIRD

I trusted you like the way birds do
When they sleep in the branches of coconut trees,

But I almost forgot, I am not a bird
Nor you a tree,

How can I be so foolish? I believed in everything
Forgetting everything, I dance and sang like a bird

But as the dawn arrived, all my dreams sway
Making me atone,

I am not a bird nor you a tree!

LOVE!

If I showed?

I knew;

It would be kiddish!

If I Hide?

I knew;

It would slowly kill me!

I showed and felt mocked,
I Hide and I suffered;

Love!

BELOVED!

I am a dreamer and thou art my dream
I am a mad and thou art my madness

I am a wanderer and thou art my destiny
I feel thee! And thou art my feeling,

Let the bell toss, let flowers
Fall on thy feet,

May birds, crickets, butterflies, mushrooms
Sing the song of you, and for you...

TO THE ONE WHO IS READING

Who are you?

Not any camera can capture your beauty,

Who are you?

Not any poet can pour you in poetry,

Tell me, where are you from?

Why I feel like I found myself;

In your sweet company!?

TO EMPATHS

You may cry in the mid of the night
Wondering life that kills you every day,

Life may slip out of your hand
You may feel dead albeit you breathe,

You may try to feel alive but end up making
Fools of yourselves every time,

You may feel stupid and blame yourselves
For treacherous voyage that comes your way,

But if you stand not giving up
Not losing your voice within,

Not fading your purity even after
Getting strangled in the web of absurdity

You will end up being, where you should,
You will end up being,
Who you really should be,.
Trust the process.

If life is a dream, I pray
May you wake like a dawn,

Like a new-born baby
With the chirps of Cocks and birds;

Singing in the golden ray of new sun
In the merry of new sunlight;

May its warmness melts
Your frozen heart and soul.

THE ISSUE OF MULTIDIMENSIONA BEING

There is poet inside me, fighting
Every day to be a poem,

There is vexed musician Playing same old boring chord

.There is juvenile longing to be free,
And there is an old man conflicting and screaming:

It is better to save self from this world
Than to save this world
&

There are monks laughing
With all the turmoil going on,

And there is me witnessing everything

What a beautiful tragedy!

IT IS NOT TEARS, MY DEAR

It's a pearl!

Fool he or she maybe be;
To expect such love:

In the world of machines;

Like of Laila and Majnu
Radhe and Krishna
Shiva and Shakti

But don't you think?

It is better to be a fool
In love than loveless?

.I can feel she is coming shimmering
Like glitters in the Ganga;

I can feel her vibration in the beating of my heart
Sounding like the chariots of hundreds of horses,

Tossing billions of bells inside my head
Like the songs of crickets, like the clatters of waves,

But deafening silence hung in the air,
Like mysterious virus(corona);

So, I secretly whisper to God through my poems
To let she know, I wait for her like the way

Fish waits for water in the desert.

To **Ashw..**

ONE-SIDED FOOLISHNESS

The sun goes down but it does not feel
Like a sunset anymore,

I hear chirps of the birds but it does not sound

Like a song without you,

I see blossoms of flowers but

I fail to feel its fragrance,

Day passes by and in the night

The pain ache like the stomach of a hungry and
homeless man,

Lying palely in dreadful street,

And I sleep with hope, to feel this life all over again

But I fail! I know I am breathing but I barely feel alive,

Without you and I just do not know what to do.

Everyone lives and go, yet the one
who tries to feel alive die here!

Everyone is okay to walk in the road
Where they are told, Yet the ones;

Who tries to set road get kicked here,
Everyone feels okay when they believe
What they say,

Yet the one who questions and wonder
Gets mad here,

We rush, life seems hard, spent half of our life
Running after life, Yet, we feel so unalive here.

TO THEE!

By what name, I should call you, my beloved?
I feel and find you in everything!

You come in colours of the skies
In music and in weather,

You are the scent of flowers, The flow of rivers
You flow being force,

Yet I fail to merge in you, where to go my love?
I cannot go to Kashi nor may climb the Kailash,

Nor can dive into the depths of oceans
Yet this lonely insane soul traverse

Like a homeless star, In the infinite sky
You are not here, but you are, even in this absence.

You are somewhere inside me
Like symphony playing in the streets
By homeless and helpless musicians,

Like a desolate poet rotting in a gutter,
You speak thousand stories, being in my head
Being the brain,

When thunders and lightening howls
Inside my heart, you flow being a tears
Like the rain from the sky,

Like a river you flow down my veins
In me you shine being the sun,

You exist being the mood of difference seasons
Tell me who you are and where to find you?

PROPHETIC DREAM

So many sinners waiting for death
Under the ground,

Above the ground so many
Fervent people secretly waiting

For the same fate!
Oh! What a bittersweet tragedy;

Such a sweet and sorrowful symphony,

Maybe life is so much more not just
Merely a dream or drama!

ICU

Only when your life is one breathe away,
You realize;

We cannot forget the person
Who live deep within our heart,

No matter!

Who and where we are!

OM

Maybe you are invisible,
Because you are omnipresent/potent;

If you would be visible
How our life would be?

Maybe we would definitely,

Take you for granted
like the fruitless trees?

You are hidden,
so that we seek?

You come being the twinkles of the stars
You are the scent of flowers,

Oh! my darling, you are the mystery
Hidden in the depth of forest,

Life comes through you,
You are the scent of soil,

This Life would not exist
Without you, come love

Being the light, being the rain
Let us feel you, once again!

How long we shall wait to live;
Being alive? Why cannot we kiss

Stranger in the road without
Any guile?

Bring me back to life

I burn, burns, and burned
In the flames of love,

let me burn till you turn
My pride, ego, hunger, greed, hatred
Lust into ashes,

Burn the one who I am not
And like embers,

May thy divine love,
Rise through me, being love!

And; let me live, being alive,

All over again...

OH! MAD SEEKER:
BREAK THE MIRROR!

I love dark room, without any lights
I love the silence in the mid of night;

I love rooms without any mirrors
As when I see myself in the mirror

All I see is my face, but that face is not me;
I fail to see the real me!

Maybe, what I am in the darkness
Is more me; Maybe

Darkness makes us see beyond
What/how we see ourselves in the mirrors,

Maybe darkness is the road to light!

Oh! sleepy people, oh busy youths;
Educated fools;

Sing a song, Whistle for the Sun
For the bird,

Let your joy shine through you,
If you can, do not hurt;

Dance being in tune with thy soul,
Fill the emptiness of your heart with

The love that flows in the air,
Don't you believe? Ask plants and flowers

What they consume:
They consume light of the sun,

And you?

If life is a river I would immerse deep;
Then just floating;

I would get wet from head to toes,
Stains my clothes with algae,

Crack my skin and bones just to feel life
I would accept life as a blessing but

Sometimes I wonder, I exist that is why Life exist,
Or Life exists that is why I exist?

WISDOM OF THE WISE

Read! But do not just implant what you read;
Believe! But do not disapprove, what you do not believe,

Do good but do not consider them bad, in the end
Every experience of life matter's,

Maybe the light we seek is not outside but within,
Sometimes system, society, people may drag's you down

But remember my dear,
Whole universe bows you, when you bow thyself,

When you feel the air made of light,
When you feel the love and light of thy heart.

Love of a deaf and dump poet!

No! I do not just want to have sex with you
I want to sleep naked, being a soul, being the light,

I may sing the song being a song
And may touch you, surrendering myself,

I will not mind thy sweaty skin, unwashed hair,
Stinking breath beyond everything, I know;

In the end; love shall win, love wins!

I will roll over you like colors in a blank piece of paper
Like music in a rhythm and will flow in you being a river,

Shattering all borders and boundaries, that cages us,
And then I will worship you from my heart and soul.

(CERCA TROVA)

I wanted to love, but you wanted to be liked,
I believe in vibes, but you believed
In trends and style;

I was living but I was dying,
We could be the one, but whom to blame?

Either worm that poisoned our fruit of love

Or the karma that drifted us apart,
Or the time that did not favored us?

Wish life would be a movie:

What?

What. What?

Isn't life a movie?

ODE TO LADY WHO BROKE POET HEART

You float like a dead fish in a deserted forest

Hypnotizing me leaving me all alone in a deserted forest

You were my light!

I long to long to see the brightest eye

I miss thy sweetest scent;

Since you left:

I followed thy like a lost puppy

In some kind of carnival fair

I got on my knees on the ground

And I pray thee?

And thee said don't dance like a snake,
Rather be a snake charmer; My comrade!
And I asked thee where is she?

NOTE BY A PERSON WHO WAS ROTTING AND PEOPLE WERE LAUGHING!

It's not easy! I know, it's not easy to be me, and especially it's hard when you are a W-I-P Artist.

You have to make fool of yourself in front of fervent and greedy people.

In this big and high buildings corrupted stairs made by money mongers,..

You have to ask for a drop of water like fish in the desert. Still some laugh at you and some give a damn, but let them!

Because I believe that death is a door to another life..

Rubendra kaushik Bagdash

www.ingramcontent.com/pod-product-compliance
Lightning Source LLC
Chambersburg PA
CBHW050023170726
48282CB00025B/527
9788196009700